I0417983

1

The Words of My Soul

By

Destini Taylor

This Book is Dedicated To:

My Heart, My Love, My Everything

"I always knew what you
needed before you knew simply
because the only thing we were
both lacking was each other."

- Destini Taylor

Book Description

I decided to create an experience for my audience to learn and practice self-evaluation and self-reflection. My growth derived from asking myself the uncomfortable questions so that I could learn how to be comfortable maneuvering throughout life. It is not my desire for you to just read my words. It is my desire for you to consume them and articulate them into your own using a process of asking yourself questions that allow you to self-evaluate and self-reflect. You will find these questions at the end of every chapter.

HOW TO ESTABLISH AND MAINTAIN HEALTHY RELATIONSHIPS

- Are there _changes_ you need to make in your relationship?
- Are you _blocking_ your opportunities to find your soulmate?
- Are you _holding on_ to a relationship that does not add value to your life?

SOLUTIONS:

1. **Self-Healing** through Poetic Expression
    Self-Healing through poetic expression opens up the
    door of opportunity for growth. It also allows you to
    be able to complete shadow work needed from past
    and/or current trauma that you have experienced.
    You will notice the level of vulnerability the author
    demonstrates as she expresses her internal pain
    from past experiences and the unconditional love
    she expresses for the love of her life. **Self-
    Reflection** through Internal Research
    Self-Reflection is a vital attribute to have in order to
    prevent stagnancy within self-growth and the
    growth of your relationships. It is important to
    research past goals, old writings, social media posts,
    etc. in order to take accountability and understand
    your previous mindset and any adjustments you've
    made that correlates with your current mindset. The
    author does this by including a "Comments by the
    Author" section after each and every poem.

2. **Self- Evaluation** through Thorough Analysis
    Once you have practiced self-healing and self-
    reflection, it is imperative to self-evaluate. The
    evaluation process means being able to take
    accountability for your previous mindset and the
    changes you've made that factor into your current
    state of mind. The author takes you through a

timeline of the mindset she had before she met the love of her life along with the development of her mindset during the course of the relationship.

WHAT OTHERS ARE SAYING ABOUT
"The Words of My Soul."

5.0 out of 5 stars **Boundless Honesty an awakening**
Reviewed in the United States on February 7, 2021

5.0 out of 5 stars **Impeccable Read!** This book exemplifies true love in its purest form!
Reviewed in the United States on February 18, 2021

5.0 out of 5 stars **Finally a WOMAN who understands MEN!!!**
Reviewed in the United States on July 10, 2021

5.0 out of 5 stars **Read this if you want Long Lasting Relationships**
Reviewed in the United States on July 10, 2021

5.0 out of 5 stars **Everyone Needs to read this book.**
Reviewed in the United States on June 26, 2021

5.0 out of 5 stars **A great experience for a Higher Conscious state of mind**
Reviewed in the United States on July 10, 2021

Table of Contents

Preface

Understand the Why

I published this book with the intent to inspire men to be kings and women to be queens.

My purpose is to help you transform your mindset so that you can have the best possible outcomes in life and love.

What is the "WHY" behind my purpose? What inspires me to write, focus, and constantly find ways to elevate myself? My family. It is my duty to be the best version of myself as a mother, a partner, and as an individual. If I'm not doing that, not only am I failing them, but I am also failing myself.

I manifest wealth, happiness, growth, and freedom for my family. Every time I act towards my purpose, it solidifies my manifestation. I speak into existence that we are wealthy, happy, constantly growing, and free.

Introduction

The Naked Truth

Two people can be fully clothed and hold each other without a single adjustment in their clothing and although it is preferred that both people should be naked in order to make love, it is possible for one to be naked while the other is still fully clothed. However, nothing can start and nothing can finish without an adjustment to an article of clothing.

People remove their clothes by choice. You can't force them to take off their shoes if they are not willing to do so. You can ask for them to be removed before entering your home and they can either oblige or decline your request. You can invite them in from the cold and ask for their coat several times and they can decline and tell you they are still cold, or they are fine. They are comfortable with their coat on. If you just wait patiently, serve them tea, give them great conversation, and make them laugh and feel comfortable, you will find that in their time, at their own pace, they will remove the coat.

I am comfortable being naked and although it may be a cold day, or the sun may burn my skin, it is my choice to be content in my own skin revealed for whomever I want to see it. I made a choice to show you my skin and to the world you may be fully clothed, but I've seen the adjustments you've made at your own pace. You can keep on your coat until you feel comfortable and trust I will not force you to remove it. That is your choice to do so, but when you are ready, I'll hang it up for you.

The moral to the story is this... Some of us have walls, some of us have bridges, and some of us have a street with signs leading straight to our hearts. However, the choice to make the adjustments to remove the walls, bridges, and street signs to our hearts, are our own. Walls keep everything out, but they also prevent things from getting in. Choose your walls wisely and remember you are the builder and the breaker. The choice to do one or the other is completely up to you.

Comments from the Author

I don't presume to know all the answers. I can only speak from my personal experiences. I can tell you that one of the things I have mastered throughout my life is patience. It takes patience to love, to find love, and to keep love. When you do find it, it is definitely worth the wait. We are not all made the same and therefore, we cannot be treated the same. What happened with someone in your past does not have to be the determining factor of what happens in your future.

Allow people the opportunity to feel comfortable enough to take off their coat. Maybe they don't drink tea, but did you try offering coffee as an alternative before you just gave up? Think of how many opportunities have been missed simply because there was not enough patience present to give people the opportunity to warm up and want to take off their coat. Now that's the naked truth!

A Time for Reflection

Think of a time where you were interested in getting to know someone and that person was equally interested in getting to know you.

How long did it take before you felt completely comfortable around this person?

What are some of the things that made you feel comfortable?

How long did it take before the other person felt completely comfortable around you?

What are some of the behaviors of the other person that made you feel he/she was completely comfortable?

Chapter One

A Message from My Heart

Puddle of assumptions cause they couldn't read you
Silent words missed, safe behind a kiss
You probably stopped talking cause
they didn't believe you,
accusing you of that, accusing you of this

But you don't have to talk because I can see you clearly
and I don't ask for promises, I go with how I'm feeling
Ever since I met you I could see
it in your eyes, connected with your smile,
impressed by your style

And when we hit the dance floor for the first time
I kissed your soft lips hoping soon you would be mine
I knew you had some drinks
and I didn't want you to drive home,
so I said you could come with me and sleep until the morn

I hope your first impression wasn't that I was a hoe
Like how can she trust someone she doesn't even know
Let me set it straight you were the first and you're the last
I'm sure that you've discerned that I'm a woman full of
class

With the space that I was in I felt like meeting you was fate
I ceased the opportunity before it was too late
It wasn't about sex, from day one I showed I cared
I was asking about your needs and trying to be there

Chemistry inevitable like this was meant to be
Definitive reasons I'm with you
and clarity why you are with me

Obstacles will come my love and obstacles will go
But when it's something real you just have to let it grow
I hear what you don't say, I feel what you convey
I never will assume, I'll ask if I'm confused
I'm completely in, the root of the tree
I believe in you just please believe in me

∞∞∞∞

Comments from the Author

Have you ever met someone that takes you completely out of your character? You get so caught up in the moment and that euphoric feeling you've never felt before that you just go with it? The next day comes, and you're replaying last night's events in your head and start to become mortified of what that person you had such a connection with might think of you? Well I have good news and bad news.

Let me give you the bad news first. The bad news is you cannot control what someone else is thinking. You can go through the story of what you don't normally do, that this was a unique circumstance that occurred, and so on and so forth, but whatever seed was planted, is planted.

The good news is time reveals your character and therefore will determine how that seed grows. Besides, it takes at least six months to be able to discern if the person you meet is in fact that person. I can't begin to tell you how many people I thought I was meeting and then they took a hiatus and left some idiot in charge. I was this caged and broken person that had just removed the chains before I met the person who inspired these words. I was getting to know the person he was getting to know at the same time. How can you explain to someone you just met about who someone YOU just met is? How can you explain a feeling that you have never felt? You can't and that is exactly my point!

A Time for Reflection

Think of a time where you made a bad first impression on someone you liked.

Do you feel you were judged incorrectly?

Were you given the opportunity to change that person's perspective of you?

What steps did you take in order to change that person's perspective?

How long did it take for you to change that person's perspective of you?

Chapter Two

Hard Decisions

Leave because your heart will stay and love will overcome
Stay so I can prove to you that I'm indeed the one

Leave because you're coming back and this is not goodbye
Stay because my love is real and this is worth the try

Leave if inside your heart I'll stay and you won't let me go
Stay so we can have a chance to see how this will grow

Leave, but later send for me I'll stay right by your side
Stay and have a little faith that God will be our guide

Leave the state, but don't leave us no matter how many
miles
Stay cause when you're with me all I ever bring are smiles

Leave cause I support your need to be a better man
Stay because I do believe that fate gave us a chance.

∞∞∞∞

Comments from the Author

Did you ever think that you knew what love was and then someone came along and showed you that whatever definition you thought you had for love, was not love at all?

It was not until the very thought that what I had found was about to be removed, that I discovered the true meaning of love. It is a pure emotion with no judgment that exudes happiness at the highest level. This is the emotion that you fight for because you don't know if you will ever run across it again. I was fighting for love when I wrote those words. I suggest that if you ever come across this emotion that gives you an endless smile, allows you to be yourself, and time never fades, hold on to it and fight to keep it.

During the time I wrote this poem, there was a possibility that he would have to leave the country for work. We had only been dating for a couple of months, but I already knew he was my soulmate. I knew that I loved him and if he did in fact have to leave, I had to plant the seeds of our future with three words. He would hear the words "I love you" from me and through consistent action, he would know my words to be true.

A Time for Reflection

Think of a time where you really liked someone and you were scared to tell that person how you feel.

Why were you scared to say how you feel?

Have you ever missed the opportunity to tell someone how you feel?

If so, how did you miss that opportunity?

What are the advantages/disadvantages of telling someone how you feel?

Chapter Three

How Do I know

How do I know it's real, these feelings that I feel
These emotions that run so deep, depriving me of my sleep

How do I know it's not an attraction
Simply a chain reaction
An infatuation, imagination,
The remains from physical satisfaction

How do I know that it's different
Reality or something invented
What have you done to secure my trust
Why am I so dedicated to us

You look at me like I genuinely matter
Not like an object or something to shatter
Not like a thing you toss in the trash
Not like a punching bag when you're mad

You hold me like I am a prize
Always sincerity in your eyes
You ask about my day
Make me feel missed when I'm away

You accept me for who I am
You don't pretend to be my friend
You keep a smile upon my face
You give my child a warm embrace

You appreciate what I do
You don't treat me like I owe you
You are my blessing from up above
Created by God for me to love

∞∞∞∞

Comments from the Author

I was actually crying when I wrote those words. I realized the importance of being around someone based on the conscious choice he or she made. That person is not judging you. You can put on anything you have in your closet and that person will still look at you with adornment.

I was winning when I met him. He brought sunshine to my life and then love flowed through me. Imagine being in a relationship with someone that finds it offensive for his girlfriend to look up when another man is talking to him or finds it offensive for a woman to wear anything other than baggy sweatpants and sweatshirts that were three sizes too big or finds it to be disrespectful to wear anything pink, which happens to be my favorite color in addition to the color purple.

Imagine holding the most important treasure in your arms, walking away from someone that betrayed your trust, and you feel a push come from behind that causes you to drop your treasure as you both fall to the floor. Imagine being the only person in a relationship working day in and day out to come home and find your partner has betrayed you in ways you can no longer speak about.

I met him during a time when I was angry. I was angry at life, at love, at men, and I just wanted to have fun again. I wanted to wear clothes that actually fit me as I was 50 pounds lighter. I wanted to be free from judgment and disrespect. I wanted to be free from the expectations that had been placed upon me by others. When I met him, laughed with him, and danced with him, I felt alive and free for the first time. I smiled so much and I haven't stopped smiling since that night. That is how I knew I loved him. That is how I knew that I had never experienced what love felt like until him. He was complex, but loving him was easy.

It felt like we were two wild and free horses running together infinitely and it still feels that way. We all have these instincts within us telling us when things are wrong and when they are right. It's not too often that we want to listen when we are told not to pass go, or not to collect two hundred dollars, but ultimately we know the right decisions to make even when we don't want to make it. I did not listen to my instincts before I met him, but I was ready to listen now. Falling in love with him was the right choice.

A Time for Reflection

Think of a time where you allowed yourself to be in a friendship or relationship with someone that did not treat you well.

What made you stay in that situation?

How long did you stay in that situation?

How many of these types of situations have you been in?

Are you currently surrounding yourself around people who add value and reciprocity to your life? If not, why not?

Chapter Four

I Feel Drawn to You

I feel drawn to you in more ways than one
Your smile, your laugh, and your presence give me peace
The authenticity of our connection against all odds,
is what puts my mind and heart at ease

I have no doubt that when I need you, you will be right
there,
with no questions asked and no subconscious debates
The feeling is mutual, which I've consistently proven.
Relinquishing all of me for you to take

When my body is next to yours I crave your affection
Wrapped in your arms, you give me comfort and protection
I want you every day in every single way
Your heart is the only place I'm willing to stay

∞∞∞

Comments from the Author

It is true that I was drawn to him. Not in the sense of being clingy, but definitely in the sense where I felt constantly intrigued. He was not the type to use terms of endearment. He was not the type to tell you exactly what you wanted to hear. In fact, he was the type to tell you the complete opposite.

I was drawn to him because I had already experienced people telling me what I wanted to hear versus the truth. He was my truth and I vowed to always be his. I was and have always been a person he never had to question or doubt. I'm still drawn to him.

A Time for Reflection

Think of a time where you felt connected with someone.

What made you feel connected to this person?

What made this experience different from previous experiences?

Chapter Five

Who Are You?

You are my smile
You are the light in my eyes
You are the beat in my heart
You are the lyrics to my songs
You are the friend I trust
You are the man I adore
You are my heart, my love, my everything…

∞∞∞∞

Comments from the Author

You should never allow your past to prevent you from love opportunities. We all have a past and we all hold the reigns to our future. Some people may have experienced more tumultuous situations than others, but the fact remains that what we should take from these past situations are the lessons, not the baggage.

In this poem I was completely focused on what I had directly been shown. I was not concerned about an experience that was not mine, nor a pain I did not bear. I was focused on being in the moment. I was focused on the now. You want to deviate from thinking about who a person may or may not have been with someone else. You have to focus on who that person is to you right now. This is the best way to ensure that you stay the course. When you can only envision what someone was, could have been, or could be versus who and what he/she is to you in the current moment, it then becomes the beginning of the end for the two of you. Focus on who a person is to you now and it should give you great comfort. If it doesn't, you have some questions that you need to ask yourself about your current situation.

When you make a conscious effort to avoid the reality of who a person is now and focus on what was or what could be, you are compromising your happiness for an illusion. Who he is and what we are together always gives me comfort.

A Time for Reflection

Think of a time where you were in a relationship with someone that had a complex past.

Did you allow this person to share his or her past with you without judgment?

Did you hold things that you discovered about this person's past against him or her?

Have you ever compared yourself to someone in your significant other's past? Why?

Who is the best at being you?

Chapter Six

You Dominate My Dreams

You dominate my dreams in such a good way
Being in your arms soothes me everyday

You're not one to say this, but I know I'm in your heart
And the chemistry keeps us from being apart

Debonair in your style, hypnotized by your smile
Secure on your chest so I lay there awhile

The light in the darkness, you always shine through
With each day I'm deeper in love with you

∞∞∞∞

Comments from the Author

He did indeed dominate my dreams. He became abundantly present. His roles of a protector, life-time partner, lover, and friend were always consistent.

My subconscious mind had already figured out a way to manifest the outcomes of my conscious mind. Over time through dreams, consistency, and action my conscious mind had perfected the concept of speaking and thinking in outcomes and solutions. This all started the day I wrote this poem.

At this point, I was already made aware of his conquests and experiences that shaped his train of thought, but you know who made me aware of that history? He did. I didn't look for anything outside of who he was to me and in doing that, I was able to speak and think in the outcomes I envisioned, not based on what I wanted, but simplistically based off of who we were and still are to each other.

A Time for Reflection

Think of a time where you wanted something really bad.

What did you want?

What steps did you take to get what you wanted?

Why did you want it so badly?

Chapter Seven

Reality Sets In

Awakened by the thought of you next to me
I open my eyes to a great reality

Randomly I kiss your shoulder, your back, or your cheek
Because the words I could convey I choose not to speak

I wonder if you feel the energy behind my touch
My heart is invested, but you don't know how much

I promise to keep you happy, I won't let you down
Your heart is always safe whenever I'm around

∞∞∞∞

Comments from the Author

To keep things simple. My reality was this. I was in love. I could feel his vibes, his thoughts, and his overall energy by his touch. Later you will come to find that I learned how to feel these things simply by looking into his eyes.

Only a king could allow me to feel this way. Only a king could remove all areas of doubt. I would privately address him as my husband and publicly recognize him as my king. Reality set in...

A Time for Reflection

Think of a time where you felt a strong connection to someone.

What type of energy did you feel when you were around this person?

What did you see when you looked into the eyes of this person?

Chapter Eight

Love for a King

I love taking care of you and treating you like a king
My love has no conditions, it doesn't cost a thing

I love to make you laugh, I love to see you smile
It's effortless to love you and go the extra mile

I look forward to rubbing your back
when you've had a trying day
I truly love to serve you in every single way

Should you ever feel weak I promise to be strong
You mean the world to me, you are my favorite song

∞∞∞∞

Comments from the Author

When you are in a relationship with someone, not only do you love this person, but you genuinely enjoy the company of one another. It's effortless to do things for and with that person because it gives you joy. The other part of that is having a partner that appreciates your efforts and does not take you for granted. I know the difference because before I met him, I allowed myself to be in scenarios where I was neither valued nor appreciated.

Naturally I am nurturing and catering, but when you mix that in with a genuine "thank you" from your partner, it gives you an additional interest in finding more ways to give love to your partner without ever feeling as though you have compromised who you are as a person, or your beliefs.

Love for a King was the result of the unconditional love I have for him. He truly is my partner and my best friend.

A Time for Reflection

Think of a time when you were with someone and you couldn't stop smiling.

Who were you with?

What made you so happy about being with that person?

Is this person still in your life?

Why or why not?

Chapter Nine

Waking Up to You

Waking up to you is like the sun appearing after the rain
It's the feeling of accomplishment,
it's the healing after the pain

Waking up to you is like Heaven, a place filled with bliss
It's that gift of discernment showing love does exist

Waking up to you is the pleasure
of my best friend by my side
The one I share all my secrets with and never have to hide

Waking up to you is a blessing, I stay in gratitude
The calming of your presence removes the solitude

Waking up to you is like hope for what is yet to come
When I awake and see your face I'm waking up to home

∞∞∞∞

Comments from the Author

I could feel the difference between waking up to him and waking up without him. That was when I knew that this was something real, something pure, something actually worth investing my energy into. I knew that these moments would plant the seeds for our future together.

It is true that I knew this way before he did. He was still deciding what he would do with these moments. He embraced them. He was comfortable, but life for him was a series of moments that faded over time. He spent this time enjoying the beauty, but waiting for it to fade. He would eventually learn that his past experiences were no match for what we were building together. He would learn that the love I have for him is everlasting. I would be the first to introduce him to the true meaning of unconditional love. I would be the first to show him how beautiful love is when you have the right person to share it with.

A Time for Reflection

Think of all of the people you have around you.

How much energy do you invest into the people around you?

How much energy is invested back into you?

Does your energy feel drained or replenished?

Chapter Ten

What is My Type?

Asking me today, my answer would simply be you
It's not meant to impress, I'm just telling you the truth

My type before you was the loudest one in the room
No life goals, no loyalty, no substance, no cool

The habitual liar using the past as an excuse
The type to control me and emotionally abuse

The ones who exploited me and laughed at my flaws
See me broken and in tears and would just drive off

The ones who said the words I love you,
followed by actions of disrespect
The ones who showed everyone else affection,
but me, they would neglect

The type to not be at my side when I buried my father
The type to push me on the ground
while I'm holding my daughter

So now you know why I say my type is you
My past is why I notice every little thing you do

With you I'm completely naked with all my flaws revealed
So though your words are silent, I know just how you feel

My type is you...

∞∞∞∞

Comments from the Author

I was the girl that allowed people to disrespect me and create turmoil in my midst. I remember asking the universe for someone years ago, but I was not ready for him. My mate would challenge me like no other and before I could accept the challenge, I had to stop being the girl and become the woman. I had to recognize what I was attracting and seal off that door. I met him the moment this took place.

I knew he was the one I had asked for when I looked into his eyes. I asked for a man, but the universe knew I deserved a king. I knew that I could now accept the challenge of his presence. Initially I was the woman he wanted, but over time I would be the queen he needed. I knew he was my type and later he would discover that I was his.

A Time for Reflection

Think of the different people you've formed friendships with, or even past relationships with that were not good for you.

What were some of the attributes that attracted you to those people?

What do you feel attracted them to you?

When did you discover these relationships were not good to you?

What steps did you take towards removing the relationships that were not good for you so that you could make room for healthier ones?

Chapter Eleven

Building a Castle

Tumultuous memories faded
by your charismatic disposition
Mentally elated by the future I envision

Your crown, your throne, your kingdom, your lair
My crown, your queen, the approval in your stare

Our bond secured by loyalty
Bank accounts look like royalty
Foundation so solidified it outranks the majority

Power we shall have, wisdom we shall gain
Distance may delay us, but we remain unchanged

See through my eyes even if it's a moment
Love through my heart, even though it's been broken
Feel through my soul, you will know it's authentic
Wrapped in your arms I can tell you've ascended

∞∞∞∞

Comments from the Author

I always understood the concept of building a foundation. I strive to do this in my friendships and relationships. However, I didn't quite understand until recently that not everyone is meant to build with you. In fact, some of the people you keep around you will sabotage what you are creating if you give them the opportunity.

I found myself more aware, keener, and more equipped when he came into my life and with that, I began to notice my surroundings. I began to remove the loose ends and start the process of building a castle. I knew there would be some tough moments. I knew that we would face some challenges, but we would be equipped with a solid foundation to build our castle on.

A Time for Reflection

Think of a time where you were trying to build a foundation with someone.

What steps did you take towards building that foundation?

What steps did the other person take towards building a foundation with you?

Why did you choose that person or people to build a foundation with?

What helped you build the foundation?

What prevented you from building the foundation?

Chapter Twelve

Imperfectly Perfect

When I first met you I was broken
Trapped in the darkness of my emotions
Shattered by physical and emotional pain

When I first met you I was still open
Swollen from vulnerability
Adventurous in my spirit with no umbrella in the rain

When I first met you my tears had been hidden for awhile
The bruises of my heart were concealed with a smile
As I've come to know you my pain has been redirected
No longer neglected and blatantly rejected

As you get to know me, please understand my heart
Along with the parts that have healed,
there are parts still scarred

As you get to know me,
understand you're my first true love
My first true companion and the joy I've dreamt of

As we go through this together,
please know I would never lie
I will always be loyal and protect you and I

As we go through this together, please handle me with care
Cause through all of my flaws I will always be there

∞∞∞∞

Comments from the Author

Every relationship has its ups and downs and in order to stay steady through the emotional roller coasters, there is one ingredient you must have. Love. Love through your communication, love through your process, and knowledge that love makes what seems impossible, possible.

Love is truly a universal language. There is always love in my voice when I speak to him. He reminds me of a complex maze, but the love in my communication always finds a way through it. The best words I could use to describe what we have are "Imperfectly Perfect."

A Time for Reflection

Think of a time where you had a disagreement with someone that you care about.

What was the disagreement?

How long did you focus on the problem?

What steps did you take to find a solution?

Was the issue resolved? If not, what prevented you from finding a solution?

Chapter Thirteen

It's What You Do

Around you my heart has the dopest beat
You are like no other, your rhythm is unique

You give me a fire with an eternal flame
Tell me how you like it and I'll do the same

I'm never shy with you, your wishes are my command
Your desires are all in me, I oblige to your demand

You make my body shiver
when you're only two inches away
You're the last thing I crave at night
and at the beginning of my day

Your touch has so many variables
from soft, sensual, to firm
Your body is full of lessons I'm always ready to learn

You say you don't control me,
yet make love like you own me
We've already established I'm yours
so you use that power on me

∞∞∞∞

Comments from the Author

I've always found it to be true that the people you surround yourself with have the ability to bring out certain energy from you. That is why it is very important to be mindful of the people you keep close to you. In my case, it was important for me to be around people that I could be vulnerable with. As a creative thinker, I flourish in high frequencies and the more vulnerable I allow myself to be, the more creative I become.

The moment I discovered that I could be fully open to him, not be judged, and be understood, I started to see him as my husband. He became a part of my vision. I would summarize the love of my life in one word, which eventually turned into a song I wrote titled "H.I.M.E." (He Is My Everything).

A Time for Reflection

Think of a time where you felt sad, angry, happy, and loved.

Who was around you when you felt sad?

Who was around you when you felt angry?

Who was around you when you felt happy?

Who was around you when you felt loved?

Which emotion do you experience the most?

Chapter Fourteen

It Don't Always Rhyme

It don't always rhyme when you and I are intertwined
We just follow the signs
While the world is forced to read between the lines

When you and I have those conversations
So many variables in our communication
Subjects discussed with no filters and no limitation

It don't always rhyme because that implies we are perfect
We may be packaged with flaws,
but our qualities make us both worth it
I can look deep in your eyes
and confidently say you deserve this
I don't blame you when you doubt the word love because
so many times you've heard it

All the I love you's and promises not to hurt you
All the I got you's transferred to someone that's not you
All the I'll be there's through thick and through thin
All the fake lovers pretending to be friends

It don't always rhyme, but we will always make sense
My actions stay consistent
so I don't need words to convince
So when I say that I love you, you can feel that I mean it
When I say that I got you, my actions show I'm committed.

I'm here through whatever
And every time we are together
Embed in your brain
We are defining forever

∞∞∞∞

Comments from the Author

Some relationships take a great deal of patience. We all have had experiences that may have disappointed us. People will disappoint you because we all make mistakes. Some of us are in relationships with people that don't value us, while others are in relationships with people they do not value.

The best way I could tell you how to determine whether or not you should invest your time and patience into a relationship is to first assess the value you are giving and the value being added. In my case, we were both adding value to one another in a plethora of ways.

He had been disappointed, he had been manipulated, and he had been betrayed. I recognized that he had probably done his share of disappointing others, but nonetheless, he had integrity. You want to build something with someone that has integrity and I decided that he deserved my love. He deserved my patience and I would give him as much time as he needed to heal. Our love is my poetry. We don't always rhyme, but we always make sense.

A Time for Reflection

Think of the people that are the closest to you.

Name three ways that each of the people close to you adds value to your life.

Name three ways you add value to their lives.

Chapter Fifteen

Why Now

I went hunting for my happiness and embraced being me
I met you during this transition of finally feeling free

I chose you for those experiences that I had never done
You were the first choice I made to finally have some fun

You met me as a rebel doing what they said I shouldn't
I tried to ignore how I felt with you,
but found that I couldn't

So when you ask why now, my response is why not
I've had so many firsts with you and don't want it to stop

With you I'm vulnerable and open
because you make me feel protected
I can try new things with you and still feel respected

Back then there was no you and now here you are
The man I share my firsts with, the one who has my heart

∞∞∞∞

Comments from the Author

We would always have these random moments where we would talk for hours. During those discussions he would sometimes ask me questions that I would articulate later in the form of a poem. This is one of those poems.

He wanted to know why I was making the choices I had been making at this point in my life. He wanted to understand what it was about him that made me so comfortable, so free, and so open about things I had never done with anyone else. I think when you are able to answer the "Why Now" question, you become closer to having your soulmate. He was my soulmate, the one person that made every new experience beautiful. So again I say, "Why Not?"

A Time for Reflection

Think of a time where you finally decided to let your guard down and trust someone.

How did that person inspire you to want to let your guard down?

How long did it take you to let down your guard?

What was the outcome of this relationship once you let your guards down?

Chapter Sixteen

Every Time I Say Your Name

Every time I say your name it's followed by forever
Perfectly imperfect every time we are together

Tattoo is official so commitment is not an issue
This love is an investment and I plan to grow it with you

Embedded in your heart
you have me sitting nice and comfy
Connected to my soul because you are my one and only

On the battlefield I am the shield and you're the sword
If this was that series we watched
I'd be your lady and you my lord

∞∞∞∞

Comments from the Author

We watched a popular series much later than most people, but the more we watched, the more it became relatable to what I feel for my king. To be with a king requires a great deal of loyalty, love, and respect. We may not agree on everything, but these three characteristics embedded in our foundation always remain intact.

He is my king! He will always be my king and every time I say his name it will mean forever.

A Time for Reflection

Think of a time where you and someone you love shared a moment that only the two of you know about.

What was that moment?

What made the moment special?

How often do you remind each other of that moment?

Chapter Seventeen

You Are…

Intriguing to my mental
Complex, yet so simple
You don't always have the lyrics
So I rock to your instrumental
Omniscient of my desires
Ignition of my fire
The plethora of pleasure
Beyond what I could measure
The flame within my fire
The definition of my desire
The reflection of my obsession
The result in every lesson
The epitome of sensation
The purpose for anticipation
The one I aim to please
The heart I keep at ease
The King that I adore
You ask for some and I give more
The one who holds my heart
The one who had me from the start
The one who makes me smile
The one for which I'll go the extra mile
The one who makes me weak
The meaning of the words I speak

∞∞∞∞

Comments from the Author

It took me a long time to understand that not everyone deserves your trust, your love, your respect, and your loyalty. There are boys, there are men, and there are kings just as there are girls, women, and queens. I had always been groomed for a king because I've always held the crown of a queen. However, I had misused my crown. I was acting like a woman still holding on to girlish qualities. Men and boys have no business in a queen's lair, but I had allowed them to congregate there and utilize my gifts knowing there would be no reciprocity. Aware that they would never meet me on my level. I had disrespected my crown by behaving as a woman and sometimes, a girl. This had to change and it did.

I met him on a dating site. It is true that a picture can tell you so much about a person. I recognized who he was before I even knew him. His presence resonated with me as calm and inviting so I was the first to say hello. As I suspected, he had substance. That encounter led us to where we are now. The universe will always show you what you are ready to see and I saw him. At first, I thought he was a man, but the familiarity of his presence showed me that he was indeed, a king. He was to be handled differently and he would be worthy of my gifts.

I had decided that I would be his queen. I would heal his heart and remove his pain. My presence would eventually encourage him to leave the past behind and my love would ensure safe travels into what would be unknown to him, yet familiar to me. A queen knows how to love and protect a king, but a king is not always accepting of it. He requires time, patience, and consistency. Three elements that I still continue to give him.

A Time for Reflection

Think of a time where you felt lost, confused, and maybe even alone.

Who are you?

What defines you?

Who defines you?

What do you represent?

What do you want to be known for?

Chapter Eighteen

Sweet Subtle Kiss

Sometimes I silence the words that describe my bliss
They won't always be comparable to a sweet subtle kiss

Each kiss that I give you has a meaning attached
From your neck, to your shoulders,
stomach, chest, and back

When I say the words out loud
I don't think you can hear me
So I speak with my lips on the off chance you'll feel me

So even if you don't understand just remember this
There is always a meaning behind my sweet subtle kiss

∞∞∞∞∞

Comments from the Author

We had been apart from one another for about three months and the distance felt like sharp needles being inserted into my heart without anesthesia. I remember him standing there waiting for me at the airport and it was as if his presence had instantly repaired the punctures in my heart. He showed me around and it felt as if he had never left. We were reconnected, but when we arrived at his temporary residence, a place I would never refer to as his home, I felt an unknown presence. He needed a reminder of who I was so I gave him one, but later I would discover that I needed to remind myself of who I was as well.

I went to visit him as a smitten girl with child-like fantasies and that is not what he signed up for. He signed up for a queen that could meet him on his level and me showing up as a girl only gave confirmation of the unknown presence I had sensed the moment I stepped in that apartment. I did not recognize the magnitude of what I'm explaining to you now at that moment, but through a subtle kiss and silent words I spoke to myself I promised he would never see that girl again. When I returned seven months later, I showed up as his queen and he recognized me. The unknown presence that I once had anxiety about had become irrelevant. This time when I held him, I silently said the words "I flow into you and you flow into me," three times and I sealed those words with a subtle kiss.

A Time for Reflection

Think of a time where you either spoke too soon, too much or too late.

What is a non-verbal way that you could have expressed gratitude?

What is a non-verbal way that you could have expressed understanding?

What is a non-verbal way that you could have expressed remorse?

Chapter Nineteen

A Queen's Cry

Mind, Body, and Soul
Craving for you to hold
Tears down my cheeks
because this bed feels so cold

Long distance is nonsense
Although love maneuvers through it
Anxiety from wanting to see you now
But I'm following your lead while we do this

Anniversary in a few days
June 25th and I'm amazed
Cause when I met you, you were leaving
Now I see you're here to stay

Don't worry I'm holding you down
Although sad, I maintain the crown
And eventually the sun will shine
Whenever you come back around....

∞∞∞∞

Comments from the Author

One of the most challenging obstacles for us was when we knew he would have to go overseas. He was only supposed to be gone for one year. My heart still dropped because this man was truly my partner, my king.

As time went on, I realized that we needed this. I realized that he and I were a unit and there were things that we needed to develop individually in order for us to grow to our full potential. It was in his absence that I realized how strong we were together and how much growth we needed individually.

I was always committed to him, but I had to remember to also be committed to myself. He was committed to him, but he had to learn how to be committed to me. The world was not going to be on our side. There would be things and people present that would try to break our bond, destroy our foundation, and we needed to both understand one another in order to survive.

Here we are, stronger than ever, and ready to take on the world.

A Time for Reflection

Think of a time where someone depended on you to hold things together and be strong.

What was one of the most painful moments in your life?

How did you get through it?

Have you ever had to delay bad news in order to protect someone?

Chapter Twenty

You are His Queen

You are hurt, but you are strong
You must stick to your plan
He is gone just for awhile
You will see him once again
This is hard, but you're a rock
You can make it through this storm
Your body feels cold as ice
But his love keeps your heart warm
You are lonely, but not alone
In his heart you'll always be
No more tears, fight with patience
Because you are indeed his Queen

∞∞∞∞

Comments from the Author

It would be extremely difficult for me to put into words the emptiness I felt while he was away. I knew that I had to continue to keep my vibrations high. He was in a new world, a new culture, having an entirely new experience, and my only job was to be a supportive queen.

There were several events that took place while he was away. I removed several people from my life that were not aligned with my purpose, a friend of mine passed away, and I faced a rollercoaster of challenges. The tears I cried were mostly behind closed doors.

I had to show him strength. I smiled through the pain. I sent him silly videos, great vibes, and all of the support he needed to feel my love. I had to keep reminding myself, "You are His Queen."

A Time for Reflection

Think of a time where you felt insecure in your relationship.

What do you love about yourself?

What are people more likely to come to you for or ask you before going to anyone else?

What attracts people to your energy?

What can you do that most people you know cannot?

Chapter Twenty-One

I Am

I am the purest form of love,
uniquely designed to give wholeheartedly
Free will to choose and my choices include you

I am a woman of patience
One day you will break my heart
I don't know when and I don't know how,
but I expect the pain to be great
Only then will you see me for the first time
This is an inevitable process

I use the term inevitable because there are no
inconsistencies or contingencies in my love for you
Your love is complex
and not expressed naturally through words,
though within your words there is great healing, a
medicinal element I need from time to time

I am wounded
I came to you this way
I was wounded in combat for my freedom,
my happiness, and my peace

All things provided under the security of your midst
My external presence appears unscathed
to an unfamiliar eye, but my love,
you can see it if only you make the choice to look

I am random
Thoughts, words, and moments randomly surface
There is always a source
from which the randomness exudes
I assure you with every random question, statement, or
gesture, there is substance

I am open
I am a portal for what is spoken and unspoken
I can humbly ask you not to hurt me, but you will do it
anyway so I don't bother asking
You don't want to my love, but you will

You are a collector of hearts
Each heart has its own designated area, except mine
It doesn't fit like the rest do
The space isn't wide enough, or tall enough
You know that you have to make room for it and that
means you have to remove from your collection

I am yours
Knowing all of what I know, I remain committed
I am a deeply rooted tree that is able to survive the cold, the
dark, the rain, the sun, and the wind
It is not the weeds that need to be fed my love
It is the roots of the tree that require nourishment

One day you will pull the weeds
and see how beautiful the tree is
You won't care who sees it because it belongs to you
Others will want it, others will try to create a replica of it,
but this tree will only grow for you
I know who I am and now so do you

∞∞∞∞∞

Comments from the Author

I never had to question whether or not he loved me. At this point, it had become abundantly clear that I had a space in his heart. He was still holding on to his past. He was still resistant. He was used to a certain way of doing things and slowly, but surely he was venturing into unfamiliar territory. The life we were building would scare him and at any given moment I knew he would try to push me away. He would hurt me during this process. This process would cause me pain, but I would endure it.

I knew that I was going to be by his side through all of the ups and downs. I knew that we would have conversations about his time away that I had mentally prepared myself for. I was like no other woman that he had ever been with. I could handle his transparency. He was mine and I was his.

A Time for Reflection

Think of a time where it took a lot of patience to love and be loved by someone else.

In what ways did you exercise patience in order to allow yourself to be loved?

In what ways did you exercise patience in order to allow yourself to love?

What were the advantages/disadvantages of being patient?

Chapter Twenty-Two

My Position

He was not to be treated like an ordinary man
There was nothing ordinary about him at all
He was a man in the flesh,
but more importantly, he was a king
Many can love a king, but they were not fit to be his queen.

He had two sides.

A queen worthy must love both sides.
She must love him through his darkness.
She must stand by him should he ever lose his way
and hold his hand all the way home

I'm lead by that which I choose to follow
I allow him to lead and when the world gets heavy,
because it will get heavy,
I am his peace, his support, his motivation, and whatever
else he needs me to be.

I am his queen...

∞∞∞∞

Comments from the Author

One of the most important things in a relationship is to recognize and understand your position. The moment you doubt what your role is, you allow external forces to threaten the stability of your relationship. I claimed my position before he even knew what it would be.

He was a hunter, but I was not his prey. I was the queen that he would hunt for and he was the king that I would fight for. A lion can sense fear from miles away and there was no room for fear, weakness, or insecurities in our castle. He was a lion and I was a lioness. I've always understood my position and that is why I remain his queen.

A Time for Reflection

Think of a person that you are really close to.

What are some of the things you love about this person?

What are your pet peeves with this person?

What are some things this person likes to do that you don't really care for?

Would you say that this person is able to completely be himself/herself when around you?

When is the last time you showed appreciation to this person for choosing to be in your life?

Chapter Twenty-Three

Love

It's funny how one word can change your perspective
The meaning of what is said or unsaid can be subjective

More in sync than not, I already knew it was a match
Warning labels around your walls
saying not to get attached

But I stuck to your heart like glue
It's you for me and me for you

No I in team
No STOP in dream
I always recognized you king

∞∞∞∞

Comments from the Author

He used to warn me about getting attached to him. He would tell me how dangerous it was for me to love him and emphasize that his pace was that of a turtle. I was not afraid of the warnings he would give me. I knew that my love would cut through all of the red tape because it was genuine and pure.

It satisfied me that not just anyone could have his heart because I had reached a point where not just anyone could have mine. The secret to successful relationships is to accept people for who they are versus who you would like them to be.

I still accept him for who he is and he is everything I thought he would be.

A Time for Reflection

Think of a time where someone told you not to do something and you did it anyway?

What were you told not to do?

Why do you think you were told not to do it?

Do you have any regrets?

Chapter Twenty-Four

Colors

I can feel our colors of love as I lay on your chest
The color of you is beautiful,
but the colors of us are the best

Red is your favorite color and pink is mine
If your taste had a color I'd say it was lime

It's bright and ecstatic and brings a smile to my face
Your hands on my body are like a peach lace

You move me like a purple flower
that stands out in the crowd
I don't care about the other colors
because my color resonates loud

Your kiss is a royal blue so rich and so deep
Your tongue is like an orange so wet and so sweet

Your body is green built like a machine
I can taste the essence from your head to your feet

You're a rainbow of pleasure, the king of my throne
I will keep your colors safe
My heart is their home...

∞∞∞∞

Comments from the Author

I remember closing my eyes, laying on his chest, and envisioning all of the colors we made together. We always had such a beautiful aura. He would change the colors with his touch from red, to blue, to purple. I love the colors of his heart, his soul, his mind, and his body.

A Time for Reflection

Close your eyes and picture three of the closest people to you.

What color would you use to represent the peace they give you?

What color would you use to represent the happiness they give you?

What color would you use to represent their loyalty?

Chapter Twenty-Five

Subtle Submission

I love taking care of you and treating you like a king
My love has no conditions, it doesn't cost a thing

I love to make you laugh, I love to see you smile
It's effortless to love you and go the extra mile

I look forward to rubbing your back
when you've had a trying day
I truly love to serve you in every single way

Should you ever feel weak I promise to be strong
You mean the world to me, you are my favorite song

∞∞∞∞

Comments from the Author

It is effortless to be submissive to someone that you genuinely love. It always brightens my smile when I know he is pleased with me. I'm always available to him in order to ensure his needs are taken care of. I remember when he told me that I spoil him. Maybe I do spoil him, but he is a king worthy of being spoiled by me.

You cannot treat a king as you would a man, just as you cannot treat a man as you would a boy. His presence is that of a king and he deserved my submission.

A Time for Reflection

Think of a time where you relinquished control to someone you love.

Who did you give control to?

Why did you give that person control?

What did the person do with the control you gave?

Do you regret relinquishing control? Why or why not?

Chapter Twenty-Six:

Great Minds

The Mind of a Queen

You had a bad day
You came in the house and said nothing
You took off your clothes, sat on the couch and picked up
the remote
No kiss hello, no verbal hello, nothing…
You need silence to gather your thoughts so I am quiet
I pour you a drink
You need a strong one
Dinner will be ready soon
I set the drink on the table in front of you and walk away
Hmmm you needed that, but you don't want to drink alone.
I pour myself the same drink
You want me here, but you're not ready to talk
I sit beside you…"salute," I say and you pick up your drink
and say the same
You're ready to talk now and as always,
I'm ready to listen

The Mind of a King

My mind was heavy today
My patience grew thin and there was a sense of rage within
me I did not foresee
I don't know exactly what I need, but I know that I want to
be in the comfort of my own surroundings
She sees me
I don't have the words to greet her
I need to first remove my clothes from the day and
compose my thoughts
Maybe there is something on television to distract me
My stomach feels empty
She walks over towards me with a drink in her hand, but I
only see one
Her presence soothes me
I want her to…wow… she's in my head
She approaches me with another drink and sits next to me
as I hoped she would
The first word she says to me is "salute" and I hold up my
drink and repeat the same back to her
I sigh in relief and begin to tell her about my day

∞∞∞∞

Comments from the Author

It is very important to understand your partner. Often times we react based on our own insecurities, causing a situation to escalate into something completely different. How many of you played the role of the queen? You were cooking, cleaning, and taking care of your home. Your king arrives home and does not speak. Instead, he goes straight to the bedroom and shuts the door, or maybe he sits in a room adjacent to where you are and still says nothing. Some people take offense to this type of behavior. I urge you to allow yourself to see the bigger picture.

The thoughts of men lie deep within and it takes a certain level of comfortability for them to surface. In order to hear them, you must be present. You must learn and understand the nature of your partner and what your partner needs. I understand that your initial reaction could be emotional, but you must understand that the communication between a man and woman must begin with logic in order to be received.

Read the poem again and pay attention to his thoughts! He is not upset with his queen. In fact, he was looking forward to coming home and being in her presence. He was overwhelmed by his day and is within his rights to take a moment to process and enjoy the peace of his home.

Imagine if she took a different approach! Can you envision her asking him why he didn't speak right away when he came home? Can you picture her calling him rude? Sometimes the best thing that you can do as a partner is to be still. Wait!

Be patient! This is your partner. Give your partner the opportunity to embrace the peace of his home, especially if you are unclear about the events that may or may not have taken place during the course of the day.

A Time for Reflection

Think of a time where you thought someone was upset with you, but he or she was not.

What reason did you have to make you think this person was upset?

Did you ask if this person was upset with you?

Did you do something that would make this person to be upset with you?

Did you assume that you did something wrong?

What did you learn from that experience?

30 Days of Purple Motivation

Created by

Destini Taylor

30 Days of Purple Motivation

My goal is to always provide my audience with value. I have always found a benefit in manifesting the outcomes of my days, weeks, months, and years to come through words of motivation. I've included 30 days of inspirational quotes that I created in order to help you start each day. I want you to focus on surrounding yourself with people that add value to your life. I also want you to remember to add value to yourself.

Day 1

"Worrying does not

empty tomorrow of its

troubles; it empties

today of its strength."

∞∞∞∞

Day 2

"You can't expect
someone who doesn't
believe in love to advise
you about someone
you're in love with. The
soul that is unhappy will
never encourage the
heart to be happy."

∞∞∞∞

Day 3

"The devil is not always

recognizable. In fact,

almost always he comes

in the form of a friend.

Pay attention because

there are always signs."

∞∞∞

Day 4

"Just because I like you,

doesn't mean you

deserve me."

∞∞∞∞

Day 5

"People can only create problems in your life if you

allow them to. The devil will attack your

friendships and relationships. Simply smile

and walk away from the drama. The devil wants you

to be miserable, uptight, and alone.

The closer you are to being a better

person, the more the devil will tempt and attack you.

Just keep going in the right direction.

You have blessings to look forward

to at the end of the tunnel."

∞∞∞∞

Day 6

"If it's easier to assume the

worst of your friend, or

partner than to give him or

her the benefit of the

doubt, why keep using the

title "friend" or "partner?"

∞∞∞

Day 7

"Relationships are built on

trust. If there is no trust,

then there is no

relationship."

∞∞∞∞

Day 8

"Stop saying "I can't get
through this," and start
saying "I will get through
this."

∞∞∞

Day 9

"Stop saying "I'm real" and

just BE REAL."

∞∞∞∞

Day 10

"Stop saying "I don't know"

and go FIND OUT."

∞∞∞

Day 11

"Stop talking about what

WON'T work and focus on

what WILL work."

∞∞∞∞

Day 12

"Stop complaining about

going to work and

appreciate that you are

able to work."

∞∞∞∞

Day 13

"Stop posting inappropriate pictures and expecting appropriate results."

∞∞∞∞

Day 14

"Stop complaining about

life and start living it."

∞∞∞∞

Day 15

"Stop looking for love from

everybody else and start

searching for the love

within yourself."

∞∞∞∞

Day 16

"Be who you are and not what you think others want you to be. At the end of the day does anyone really care? They go home and live their lives just like you go home and live yours. So why waste time and energy trying to portray an "image" that you clearly aren't? That is for the weak.

It's time to be strong!"

∞∞∞∞

Day 17

"A woman can deal with
stress and carry heavy
burdens. She smiles when
she feels like screaming,
she sings when she feels
like crying, she cries when
she's happy, and laughs
when she's afraid. Her love
in unconditional. There is
only one thing wrong. She
forgets what she is worth."

∞∞∞∞

Day 18

"Thinking negatively is the same thing as being

negative. Out of every negative situation,

something positive can always come from it.

Sometimes all you have to do is change your mindset.

Remember a situation can always be much worse than

it appears to be. If you speak love, life, and

positivity into existence,

you will have all of those things.

It's that simple."

∞∞∞∞

Day 19

"Closed minds don't get fed."

∞∞∞∞

Day 20

"It takes a great team to

inspire a great leader."

∞∞∞∞

Day 21

"A leader that is not

receptive to feedback,

presents a situation that

remains unchanged."

∞∞∞∞

Day 22

"I'm not hiding. I'm in plain
view. If you can find me
you can have me, but if I'm
in your face and you don't
see me, just keep walking
because so will I, but in the
opposite direction."

∞∞∞∞

Day 23

"People can only do what
you allow them to do. They
can only use you if you
allow them to do so. Stop
blaming people for the
pain, hurt, and destruction
that you allow them to
create in your life. When
people show you who they
are, believe them on the
same day."

∞∞∞∞

Day 24

"Fake people can't show

you real love. Real people

don't give you fake love.

Once you figure out what

type of person you are

dealing with, you will know

the difference."

∞∞∞∞

Day 25

"Forget what they say and

remember what they do."

∞∞∞∞

Day 26

"Before you try to figure

out anything, love yourself

first. It's hard to give real

love to someone else when

you don't even know how

to love yourself."

∞∞∞∞

Day 27

"It's more important to

invest money and energy

on leaving your mark in

this world, than to waste

money and tears on things

and people that don't

matter."

∞∞∞∞

Day 28

"We can't blame others for
our bitterness. Being bitter
is a choice. Don't smile to
please others. Smile to
please yourself. Choose
happiness!"

∞∞∞∞

Day 29

"Being positive in your

actions are what makes you

brave. Any coward can tear

someone down. It takes

courage to be positive and

lift someone up."

∞∞∞∞

Day 30

"The concept of friendship

is defined when you're at

your worse. A true friend

who is upset with you will

still hold you in the

brightest light."

∞∞∞∞

Acknowledgments

To my first love, my inspiration, the most important person before anyone or anything else, my daughter, Treyanna Huffaker. You taught me the true meaning of unconditional love. I was ready to sacrifice my life for yours from the moment I knew you were growing inside of me. I am here to keep you safe, to teach you about what unconditional love feels like, and to give you the best outcome possible. You continue to inspire me as a person, a mother, and a free spirit. Every sacrifice I make is for you. My vision is to leave colorful footprints behind that will help guide you to be the best version of yourself. I love you kiddo!

I always knew writing was my passion. I kept a notebook and pen close to me at all times because I wanted to be prepared for those random thoughts and ideas. Over time I learned that my environment played a huge role in my creative flow. It was not until I turned 40 years old that I realized I had to restructure my environment and surround myself with people that added value to my life.

The first change I made was to remove myself from a tumultuous relationship that I had allowed myself to be in far too long. In doing this, I was able to unblock my creativity. I had placed myself in a position to receive the opportunities that had already been arranged for my life. I thought that I was waiting on the opportunities, but the truth of the matter is, they were waiting for me to become available. This is when I met him.

Acknowledgments cont.…

In a world unknown to me, I met the love of my life. He is the inspiration behind "The Words of My Soul." He took a position in my life that he didn't have to take. He became a father to my daughter, my best friend, my partner, and I recognize him as my king. I am eternally grateful for you Sean Jones for continuing to show me the true meaning of unconditional love. I love you!

When I met Marcia Baptiste in 2009, I had allowed myself to be in one of the worst relationships of my life. I had buried myself in a pile of insecurities and lost sight of my self-worth. Her love and support brought me back to the surface. She always encouraged me to be the best version of myself. She would always say "Des, you need to write that book," or "Des, you need to put your music out there." Well bestie, "We did it!" Thank you for being a godmother to my daughter, a sister to me, and being the definition of a best friend! I love you so much!

I met Connie Beatriz Erandi Andrade Rivera in 2006. We had an immediate connection and shortly after we met, I referred to her as my cousin and soul sister. I'd like to thank you for your amazing ray of love and light that you continuously wrap around my heart. I remember when you asked me "Why are you so afraid to launch?" You always pushed me to be great and reminded me of my purpose. Get excited! "We launched!" I love you to the moon and back!

Daddy I can feel your presence. I know that you are in Heaven smiling right now because even when I doubted myself, you never doubted me. Thank you for accepting the man I chose to spend the rest of my life with! Thank you for helping me turn my painful experiences into lessons that I am now equipped to teach others. Your smile is embedded inside of my heart and I will continue to make you proud. I love you and I miss you!

About the Author

Destini Taylor was born Tracy Taylor, from Gary, Indiana on December 6, 1977. She first showed signs of creativity at the age of four through music. She was a member of the choir at St. Timothy Community Church. At age nine she developed a talent for writing music and poetry and shortly after, moved to Merrillville, Indiana where she graduated from Merrillville High School. She attended Indiana University Northwest in 1996 where she studied Organizational Communication.

In 2006, she moved to Brooklyn, New York and this is where the name Destini was brought to life. She became a member and joined the choir at Emmanuel Baptist Church. Destini had her hand in several pots while in New York. She had a full-time job with an answering service, she worked part-time as a bartender, she did freelance work at Atlantic Records and Reality TV Network. She went on casting calls for acting and appeared in an independent film called "Fly Girls." She also did photo shoots with Saswat Pattanayak and still managed to make time for her close friends and family.

She became a mother to a beautiful star child in 2010, which inspired her to go back to school so she could teach her daughter the importance of completion. She acquired a bachelor's degree in Organizational Management and two master's degrees. The first master's degree was in

Organizational Management with a specialization in Human Resource Management and the second master's degree was in Entrepreneurship. She graduated with honors through Ashford University, now known as UAGC (University of Arizona Global Campus) and sang the Star Spangled Banner in 2015 when she received her first master's degree. She ran a call center for five years and discovered her ability to provide customized and creative solutions for businesses through multiple channels. In 2018, she began to invest her time and energy into Destini Creative Selections, LLC to bridge the gap between her corporate expertise and creative skill set.

In 2019, she started the Destini Unfiltered Movement in order to empower her audience to live in their truth regardless of what opinions others may have about it. She also created a YouTube Channel, she started the Destini Unfiltered Podcast, and expanded her creativity in an unfiltered written form that allowed her to connect with both men and women.

She would eventually create the DT Network (Destini Taylor Network) located at www.destinitaylor.com, in order to give her audience one platform to truly have a Destini Unfiltered experience.

A Special Thanks

Outside of the individuals listed in the acknowledgments, I would like to take this opportunity to thank some of the people that have had a positive impact in my life.

Although I may not talk to you every day, I want you to know that you remain in my heart and I appreciate the value that you have added to my life. You have consistently supported my writings, my music, my art, and my energy. You authentically celebrate my wins. You have seen my struggles in love and in life and have always uplifted me. I love you, I respect you, I thank you, and I appreciate you.

Richard Taylor
Joyce Leon
Arison Walton
Akanke Birmingham
Camelle Parker
Karma Campbell
Secelia "Jewell Caesar" Winkfield
Anastasia Summerlin

To My Sufi Sister in Heaven

Princess Hawthorne

You always believed that I would do great things and I'm very proud to take this moment and share it with you. I know that you are surrounded by the color yellow. I know that you have been watching over me. Rest in Heavenly Peace my dear Sufi sister. I love you and miss you so much! Get excited! We did it!

How to Connect with Destini Taylor

Instagram: @destiniunfiltered
@dt_twoms

Facebook:
www.facebook.com/thewordsofmysoul

YouTube:
https://www.youtube.com/channel/UCTFOP
d0xUOlvh-VmRzswE-Q

Websites: www.destinitaylor.com
www.thewordsofmysoul.com

Email:
info@thewordsofmysoul.com

Feedback:

Let us know how you felt about the book by leaving us a review on Amazon. Click HERE to leave a review.

ABOUT THE AUTHOR

- **Destini Taylor is a new female African American author that focuses on mindset, love, and relationships. She encourages self-love as well as being able to develop and maintain healthy relationships with others. She has been writing poetry for over 30 years, has her own publishing company called THE WORDS OF MY SOUL LLC, and a podcast called "Destini Unfiltered."**

CONNECT WITH THE AUTHOR

- **Podcast**: Destini Unfiltered (Available on Spotify, Google Play, iHeart Radio, Apple Podcast, ALL Platforms)
- **YouTube: The Words of My Soul**
- **Website:** www.thewordsofmysoul.com
- **Instagram:** @dt_twoms
- **Twitter:** @dt_twoms
- **Facebook:** www.facebook.com/thewordsofmysoul

FEEDBACK IS ALWAYS APPRECIATED: (tag us on your feedback on social media #destiniunfiltered #thewordsofmysoul #dt_twoms)

HOW DID YOU LIKE THE BOOK?
CLICK HERE TO SUBMIT YOUR REVIEW!